How to Become an Everyday Superhero

for Kids

14 Inspiring Stories to Foster Superhero Values

Coordinator: Morgan Barrett

Writers: Morgan Barrett, Kavya Sharma, Anne Moore, Juan Rodriguez

Illustrators: Mary Banks, Ming-Hui Zhang, Aryan Patel

Disclaimer: Any product names, logos, brands, and other trademarks or images featured or referred to within this book are the property of their respective trademark holders. We declare no affiliation, sponsorship, or partnership with any registered trademarks.

Copyright: All rights reserved. This book may not be reproduced in whole or in part in any form without express written permission of the publisher. Independently published. Text and illustrations copyright © 2024.
ISBN: 9798325058646

Table of Contents

Chapter 1
Courage (4)
The Day Skyler Became Super Kitty (6)

The Aura of Bravery (10)

Chapter 2
Justice and Integrity (14)
Alex and the Super Gem (16)

Mei Ling's Labyrinth Challenge (20)

Chapter 3
Altruism (24)
Splash Saves the Ocean (26)

The Heroic Helpers (30)

Chapter 4
Self-Control (34)
The Fiery Phoenix (36)

Layla the Wind Whisperer (40)

Chapter 5
Cooperation (44)
Blue Rocket and the Falling Tower (46)

The Magical Light of Zara and Nia (50)

Chapter 6
Turning Weaknesses into Strengths (54)
The Goggles of Bravery (56)

Naldala's Invisible Quest (60)

Chapter 7
Perseverance (64)
The Brightness of Darian (66)

The Day Lucía Stood Again (70)

Page 74

Download the Audio Version of This Book (in MP3 Format)

+ 30 Pages of Activities!

Introduction

Welcome to the amazing world of everyday superheroes! Do you know what makes superheroes truly special? It's not just their capes, or the ability to fly high in the sky. What really makes superheroes stand out are their super values, including being brave, helping others, and never giving up, even when things get tough.

You don't need to be from another planet or have magical powers to be a superhero. You have everything you need already inside you.

This book is like a secret map to finding and growing your own superhero values. We'll learn through exciting stories about courage, kindness, and never giving up.

So, are you ready to start your adventure and discover the superhero within you? Put on your imaginary cape, and let's dive into a world where your superpowers are your amazing values. Welcome to the journey of becoming an everyday superhero!

Chapter 1
Courage

Have you ever felt a little shiver of fear, like when you're standing at the top of a tall slide, looking down? That's okay! Courage is not about not feeling scared; it's about feeling that shiver and saying, "I can do this!"

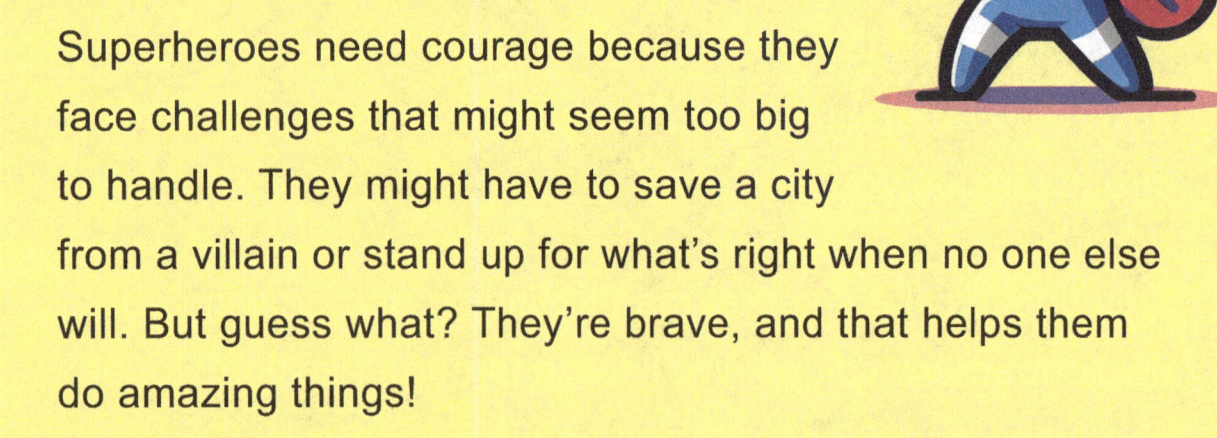

Superheroes need courage because they face challenges that might seem too big to handle. They might have to save a city from a villain or stand up for what's right when no one else will. But guess what? They're brave, and that helps them do amazing things!

Now, let's talk about you! Courage is super important in everyday life too. It could be trying a new food, making a new friend, or speaking up when you see someone being treated unfairly.

Being brave doesn't mean you're not scared; it means you try anyway, because you know you're stronger than your fear.

So, every time you feel a bit scared but decide to do something brave, you're being a superhero too. Remember, it's your courage that makes you super special and helps you do amazing things every day!

YOUR FUN CHALLENGE!

Your Mission: Find a little way to be brave. Maybe try something new you've been scared to try, like climbing a bit higher on the jungle gym or speaking in front of your class about your favorite book. And remember, even superheroes sometimes seek the guidance of wise friends or adults. Make sure to do it under the supervision or guidance of an adult.

Why? Every superhero has moments when they need to be brave. When you do something even though it's scary, you're being just like them.

Your Tracker: Here are 10 boxes. Each time you're brave, make a mark in one. Can you fill all 10?

☐ ☐ ☐ ☐ ☐ ☐ ☐ ☐ ☐ ☐

Remember: Being brave doesn't mean you aren't scared. It means you try even when you are. That's what makes you truly courageous! You're doing wonderfully!

The Day Skyler Became Super Kitty

A Story about Courage

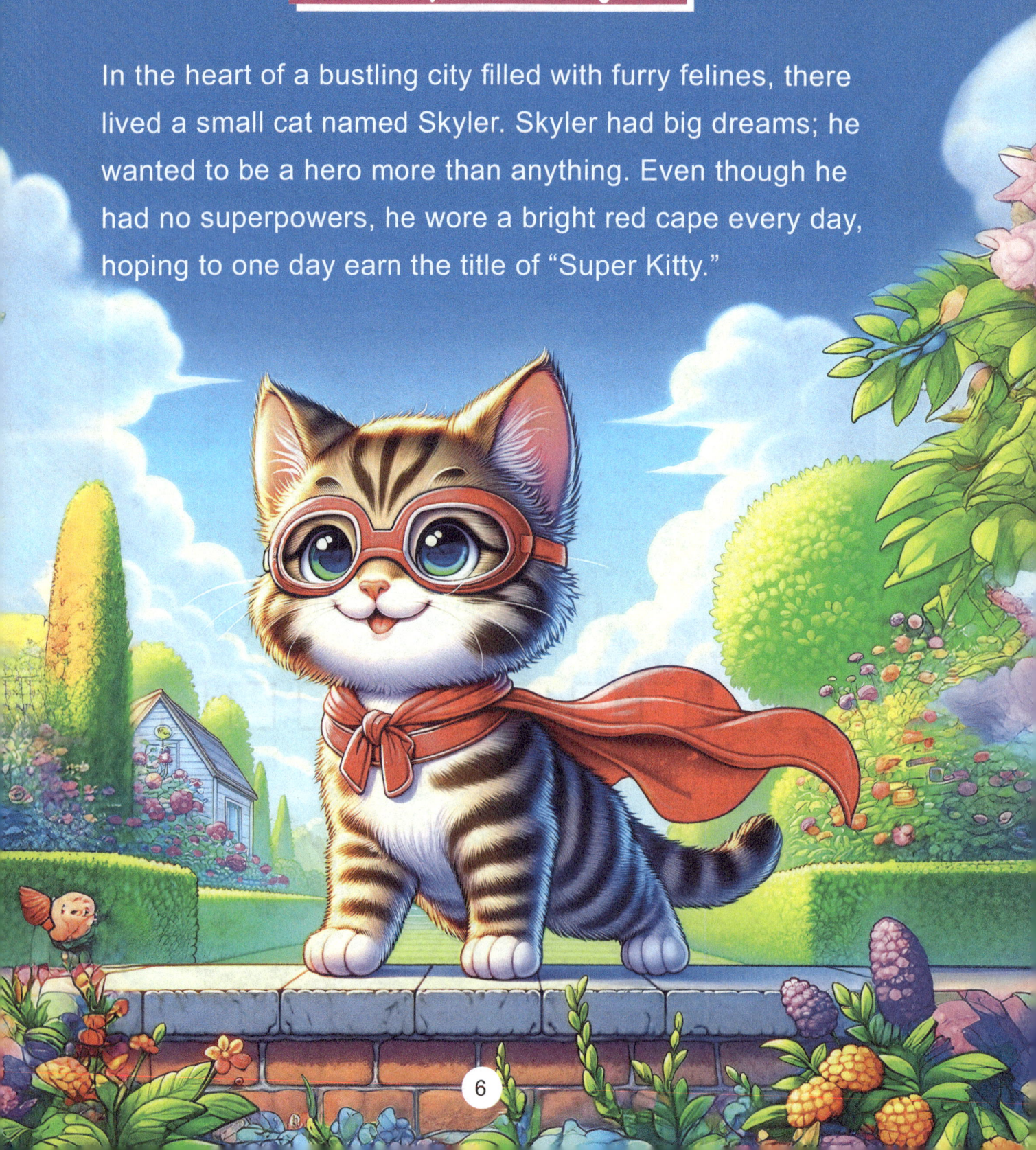

In the heart of a bustling city filled with furry felines, there lived a small cat named Skyler. Skyler had big dreams; he wanted to be a hero more than anything. Even though he had no superpowers, he wore a bright red cape every day, hoping to one day earn the title of "Super Kitty."

One sunny afternoon, a tiny kitten found herself in a tall tree, meowing for help. All the cats gathered around the tree, their tails twitching with worry. They all looked up at the kitten, then around at each other, hoping someone would brave the climb. Skyler felt his heart thump wildly. He wanted to help, but his paws trembled with fear.

Remembering his dreams of heroism, Skyler took a deep breath. He whispered to himself, "Superheroes aren't fearless; they're brave despite their fears." With that thought, Skyler began to climb. Up he went, higher and higher, his cape fluttering behind him. The other cats watched, amazed by Skyler's courage.

Finally, Skyler reached the frightened kitten. Gently, he nudged her onto his back and carefully made his way down. As his paws touched the ground, a cheer erupted from the crowd. The kitten was safe, all thanks to Skyler.

From that day on, Skyler was known not just as a small cat in a cape, but as "Super Kitty," the bravest cat in the city. His dream had come true, not because he had superpowers, but because he found the courage within himself to help others. And in the eyes of all the cats, Skyler truly was a superhero.

The Aura of Bravery

A Story about Courage

In a world sprinkled with dazzling lights and shimmering colors, there lived heroes known far and wide for their Aura of Bravery. This magical glow, a swirl of golden light, danced around only those who were brave at heart. Lila, with dreams as big as the sky, wished more than anything to have such an aura. But no matter how hard she tried, her light remained unseen.

One sunny day, while playing in the park, Lila noticed some older kids being unkind to a younger girl, their words as sharp as thorns. She looked around, hoping to see someone with the Aura of Bravery step forward. But the park was quiet, the heroes nowhere in sight.

Lila's heart pounded like a drum in her chest. She was scared, her knees felt like jelly, and she certainly didn't feel brave. Yet, something deep inside her, a voice as soft as a whisper, told her, "It's time to stand up."

Taking a deep breath that filled her lungs with the courage of a thousand lions, Lila stepped forward. "Hey, let's play nice. Everyone deserves to have fun," she said, her voice steady but kind.

At that very moment, something magical happened. A warm glow began to flicker around her, growing brighter and brighter. It swirled around her, a dazzling Aura of Bravery, for the first time visible to all.

The older kids, taken aback by the unexpected sight, stopped in their tracks. The young girl, now smiling, whispered a thank you, and the park filled with laughter once more.

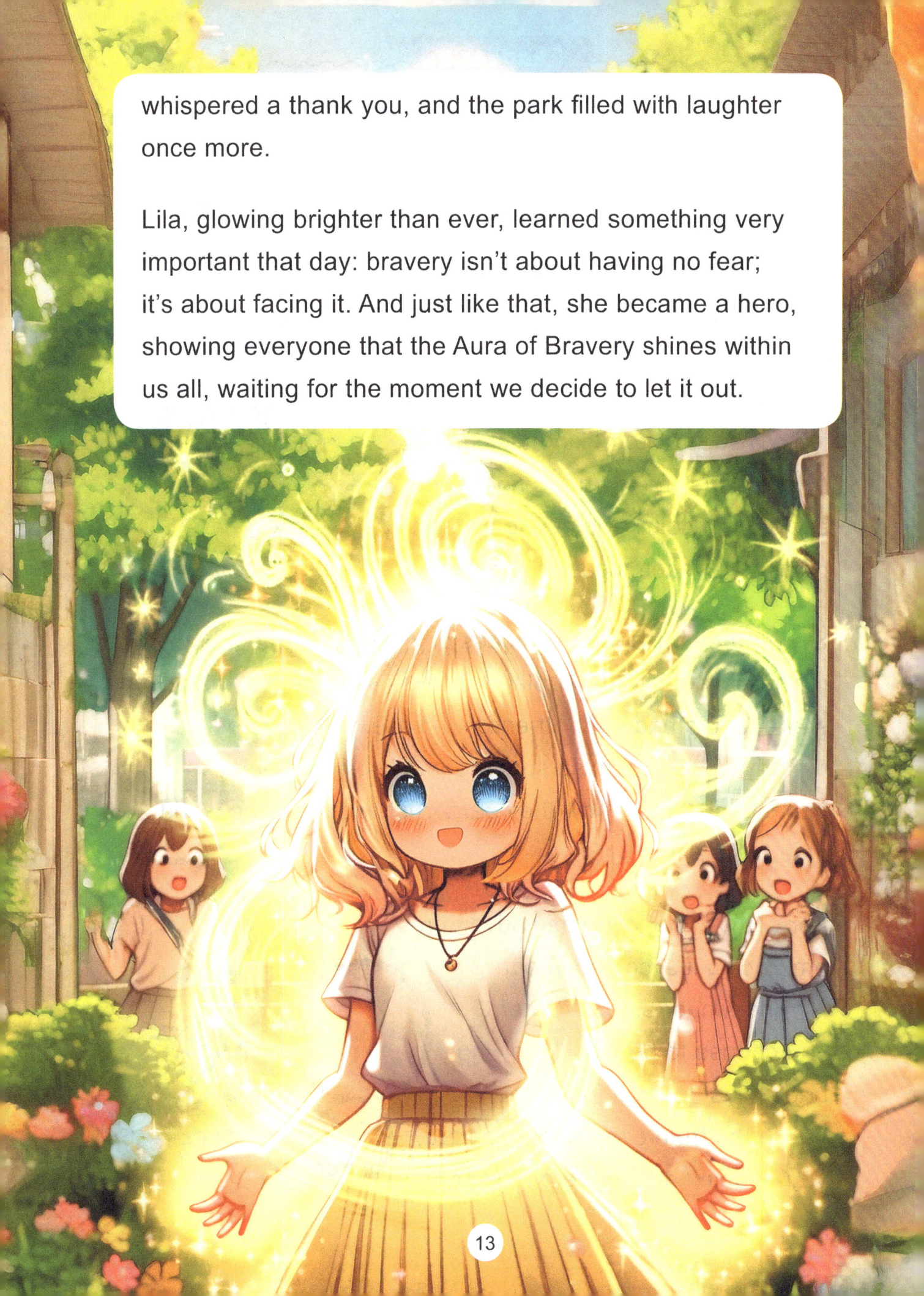

Lila, glowing brighter than ever, learned something very important that day: bravery isn't about having no fear; it's about facing it. And just like that, she became a hero, showing everyone that the Aura of Bravery shines within us all, waiting for the moment we decide to let it out.

Chapter 2
Justice and Integrity

Imagine you have a special compass inside you, not one that shows north or south, but one that points to what's good and fair. That's what justice and integrity are all about! It's like choosing to be a superhero of kindness and honesty, picking to do the right thing even when doing something a little bit naughty seems easier or more fun.

Superheroes use their compass of justice and integrity to make the world a better place. They always tell the truth, share, and stand up for friends who are being treated unfairly. Why? Because superheroes know that being honest and kind is how they earn trust and keep the world safe and happy.

For you, in your everyday adventures, embracing justice and integrity is super important too! When you choose to be fair, like giving back a lost toy you found, or telling the truth even when it's hard, you're being a superhero in your own world. That's how you make sure everyone around you feels happy, safe, and trusted.

So, remember, every hero's journey starts with the choice to do good. That's how you become a trusted superhero in everyday life!

YOUR FUN CHALLENGE!

Your Mission: Once a day, think about 3 different situations. For each situation, decide what's right and what's wrong. Say you find a toy on the playground. The right thing is to find out who the toy belongs to; the wrong thing is to keep it for yourself.

Why? This helps you learn to choose good over bad, just like superheroes. It's about being fair and kind, and that's how you become a trusted hero!

Your Tracker: Each day you think about what's right and what's wrong in 3 different situations, fill in a box. Can you fill all 10?

☐ ☐ ☐ ☐ ☐ ☐ ☐ ☐ ☐ ☐

Remember: It's all about trying to do the right thing. Even if it's tough, that's what being a superhero is all about. You're awesome for trying!

Alex and the Super Gem

A Story about Justice and Integrity

Once upon a time, in a colorful town, lived a boy named Alex who dreamed of being a superhero. But Alex had no superpowers, just a big heart and a wild imagination. One sunny day, while playing in the park, Alex stumbled upon a shimmering Super Gem hidden in the grass. The gem was lost by Lady Mighty during a fierce battle against the villainous Shadow Sneak.

With the Super Gem in his hand, Alex discovered he could fly high above the trees and shoot laser beams from his fingertips! He zipped through the sky, doing loop-the-loops, and lit up the night with dazzling light shows. For a brief moment, Alex felt like the superhero he always wanted to be.

But soon, Alex learned from the town's folks that Lady Mighty had been searching for her lost Super Gem. Without it, Lady Mighty couldn't protect the town from

Shadow Sneak's naughty tricks. Alex was torn. He loved feeling like a superhero, but he also knew what was right.

That night, under a blanket of stars, Alex made a brave decision. He flew to Lady Mighty's tower and returned the Super Gem. Lady Mighty smiled and thanked Alex for his honesty and courage. "You have something more powerful than any Super Gem," Lady Mighty told him. "You have integrity and a sense of justice. And those, my young friend, are the true superpowers of a hero."

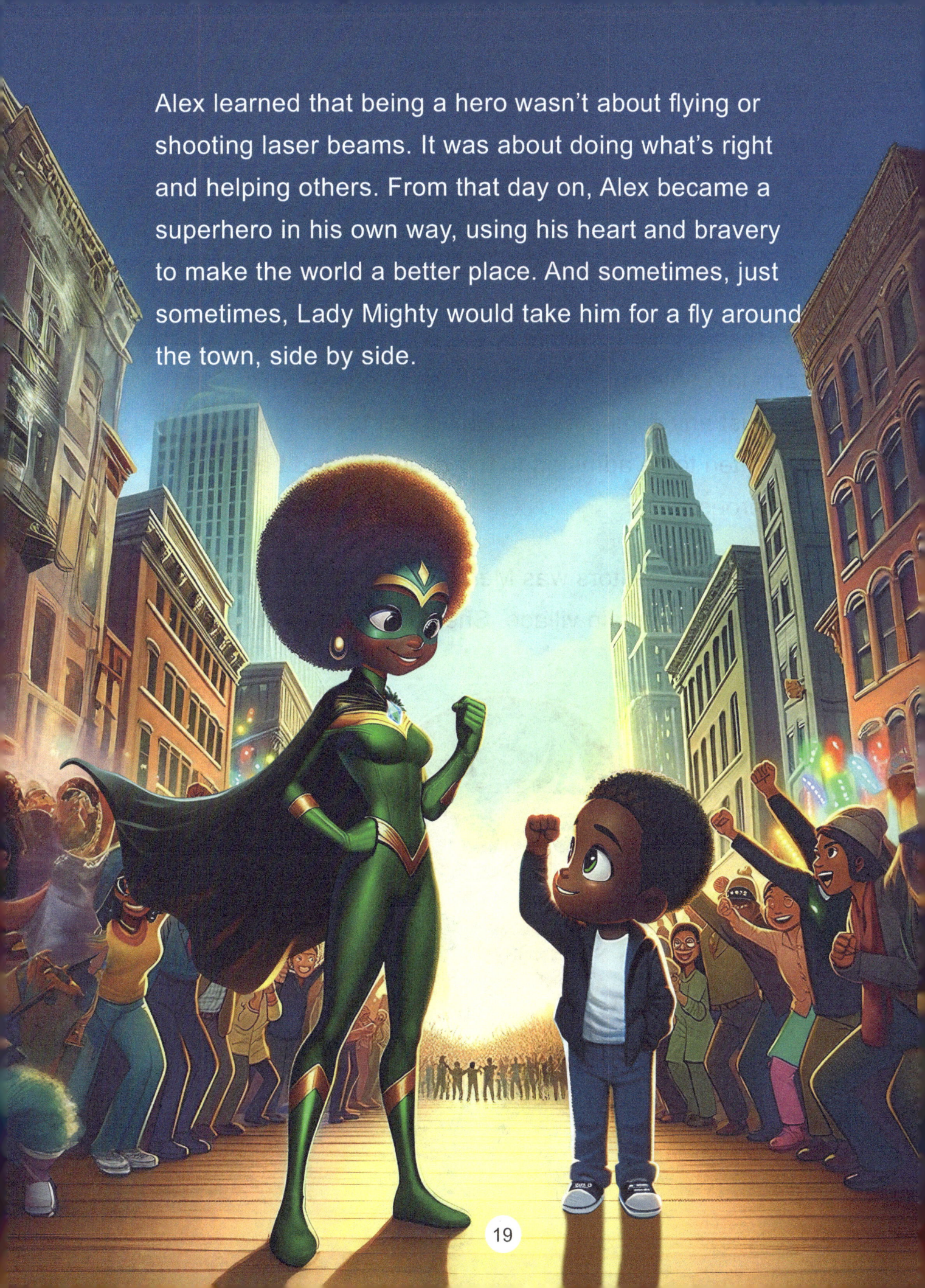

Alex learned that being a hero wasn't about flying or shooting laser beams. It was about doing what's right and helping others. From that day on, Alex became a superhero in his own way, using his heart and bravery to make the world a better place. And sometimes, just sometimes, Lady Mighty would take him for a fly around the town, side by side.

Mei Ling's Labyrinth Challenge

A Story about Justice and Integrity

Within the twisting corridors of the Superhero Academy, the annual Labyrinth Challenge was underway. This event wasn't just any competition; it was a test for all those who wanted to be admitted to the academy and become superheroes.

Among the competitors was Mei Ling, a bright-eyed girl from a small mountain village. She had prepared for months, determined to show her potential. Adorned in a makeshift superhero costume stitched together by her grandmother, Mei Ling felt ready to tackle whatever the maze held.

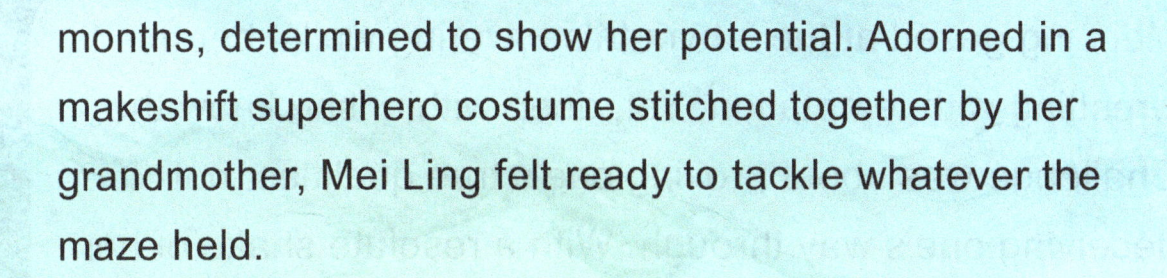

Before the race began, a fellow competitor, Jian, approached her with a sly smile. He held out a map. "This map," he whispered, "is the plan of the labyrinth, with all the paths and traps explained. Everyone uses a copy of it. It's the only way to win."

Mei Ling gazed at the labyrinth's towering walls, her mind wrestling with temptation. Yet, deep within, she knew the Challenge was about proving one's true qualities, not deceiving one's way through. With a resolute shake of her head, she refused to take Jian's map and cheat.

Navigating the maze was a whirlwind of riddles and hidden traps. Mei Ling moved with caution and cleverness, but with no map to cheat with, she emerged from the maze last. Her heart sank as she watched others celebrate their earlier arrivals.

However, the greatest twist was still to unfold. The head of the Superhero Academy stepped forward, his voice booming across the gathered crowd. The real test of the maze, he revealed, was not merely getting out of the labyrinth, but doing so with integrity. "And you, Mei Ling, by refusing to cheat, have passed the test with flying colors!"

Mei Ling emerged as the true victor, her integrity outshining the cleverest tricks. This noble choice secured her a coveted spot at the Superhero Academy. By choosing honesty over an easy victory, she demonstrated the essence of a true hero.

Chapter 3
Altruism

Imagine you have a big, beautiful balloon. It's fun to play with it all by yourself, right? But have you ever given your balloon to someone who didn't have one? That big smile on their face is what altruism feels like. It means "Others come before me." It's all about sharing, caring, and helping, especially those who need it the most.

Superheroes are super at altruism. They zoom around, not just for the fun of it, but to help others. They save people from trouble, not because they'll get a trophy, but because they know it's the right thing to do. Their superpower is their big, caring hearts that put others first.

Why is altruism important for you, too? Because being kind and helping others makes the world a happier place, just like how sharing your balloon does. When you help a friend in need, share your snacks, or even give a hug, you're being a superhero. You show that you care about making others feel good, which is one of the greatest superpowers of all.

So, let's be superheroes with our actions, by putting others first and spreading kindness everywhere we go. That's the true superpower of altruism!

YOUR FUN CHALLENGE!

Your Mission: Do one kind thing for someone without them asking. It could be as simple as drawing a picture for a family member, helping a friend pick up dropped toys, or leaving a thank-you note for the mail carrier. Even if they don't say thank you, you've done something wonderful!

Why? Acts of kindness are superhero deeds! Each time you do something kind, you're spreading joy and making the world a brighter place.

Your Tracker: Each time you perform an unsolicited good deed, fill in a box. Can you fill all 10?

☐ ☐ ☐ ☐ ☐ ☐ ☐ ☐ ☐ ☐

Remember: The most important part is that you're spreading kindness. That's what being an everyday superhero is all about!

Splash Saves the Ocean

A Story about Altruism

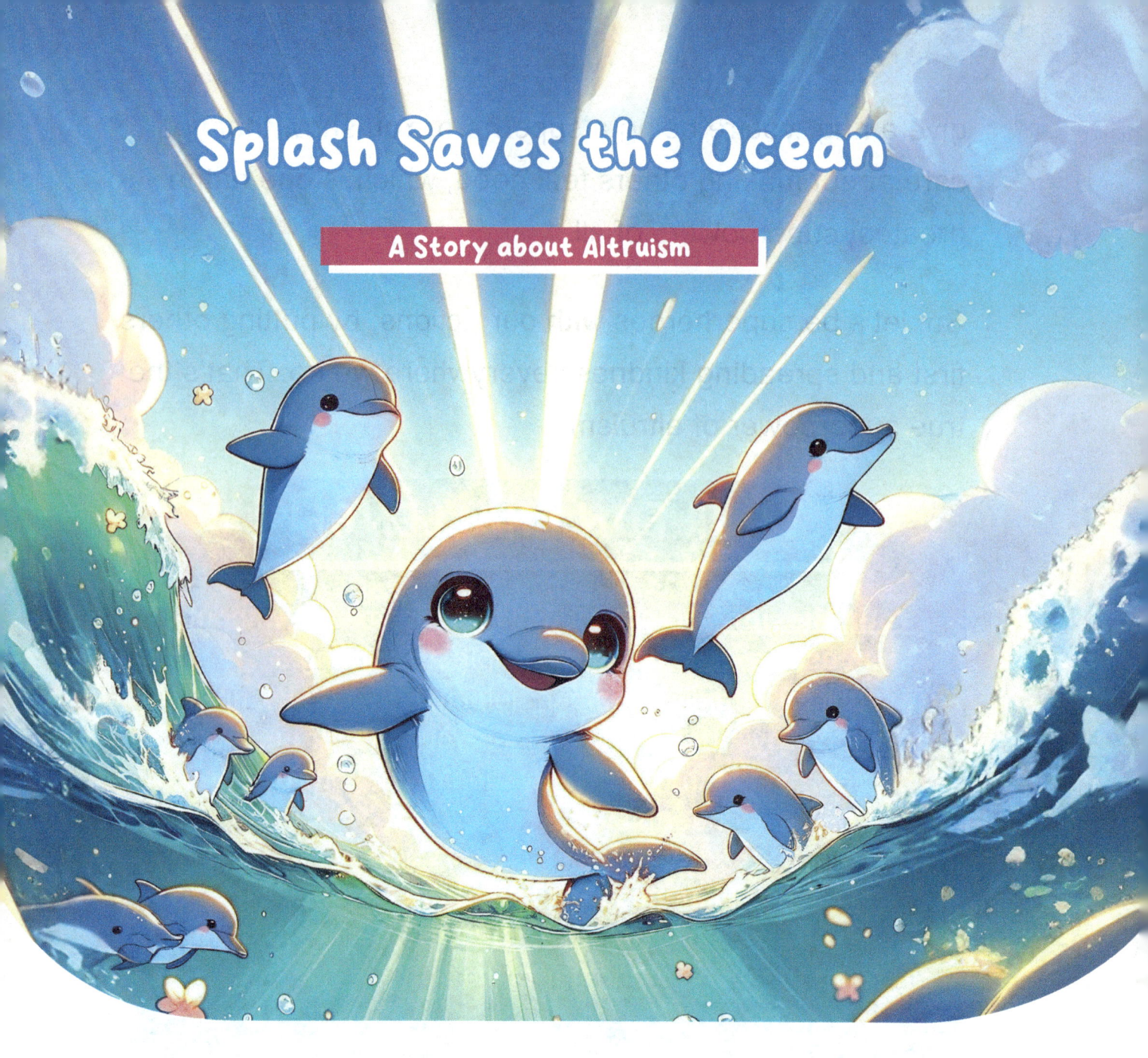

Once upon a time, under the shimmering waves of the Big Blue, there lived a playful dolphin named Splash. Splash loved nothing more than to leap and dive with his dolphin friends, chasing the sunbeams that danced through the water.

One day, while playing hide-and-seek among the coral reefs, Splash noticed something strange. Several plastic bags were drifting through their underwater home, like ghostly jellyfish, threatening the tiny fish and precious sea plants. Splash's heart sank; he knew these bags didn't belong in the ocean.

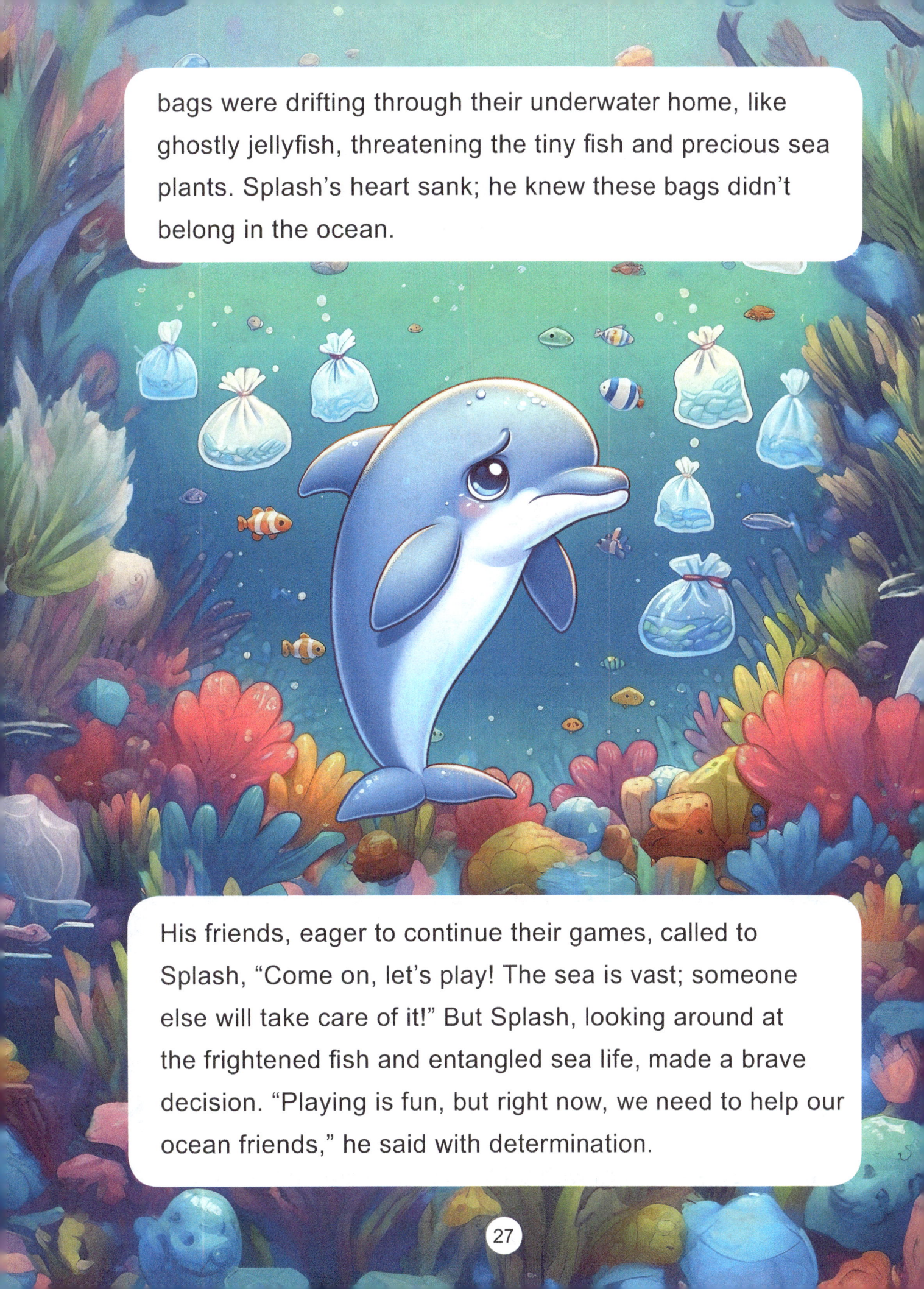

His friends, eager to continue their games, called to Splash, "Come on, let's play! The sea is vast; someone else will take care of it!" But Splash, looking around at the frightened fish and entangled sea life, made a brave decision. "Playing is fun, but right now, we need to help our ocean friends," he said with determination.

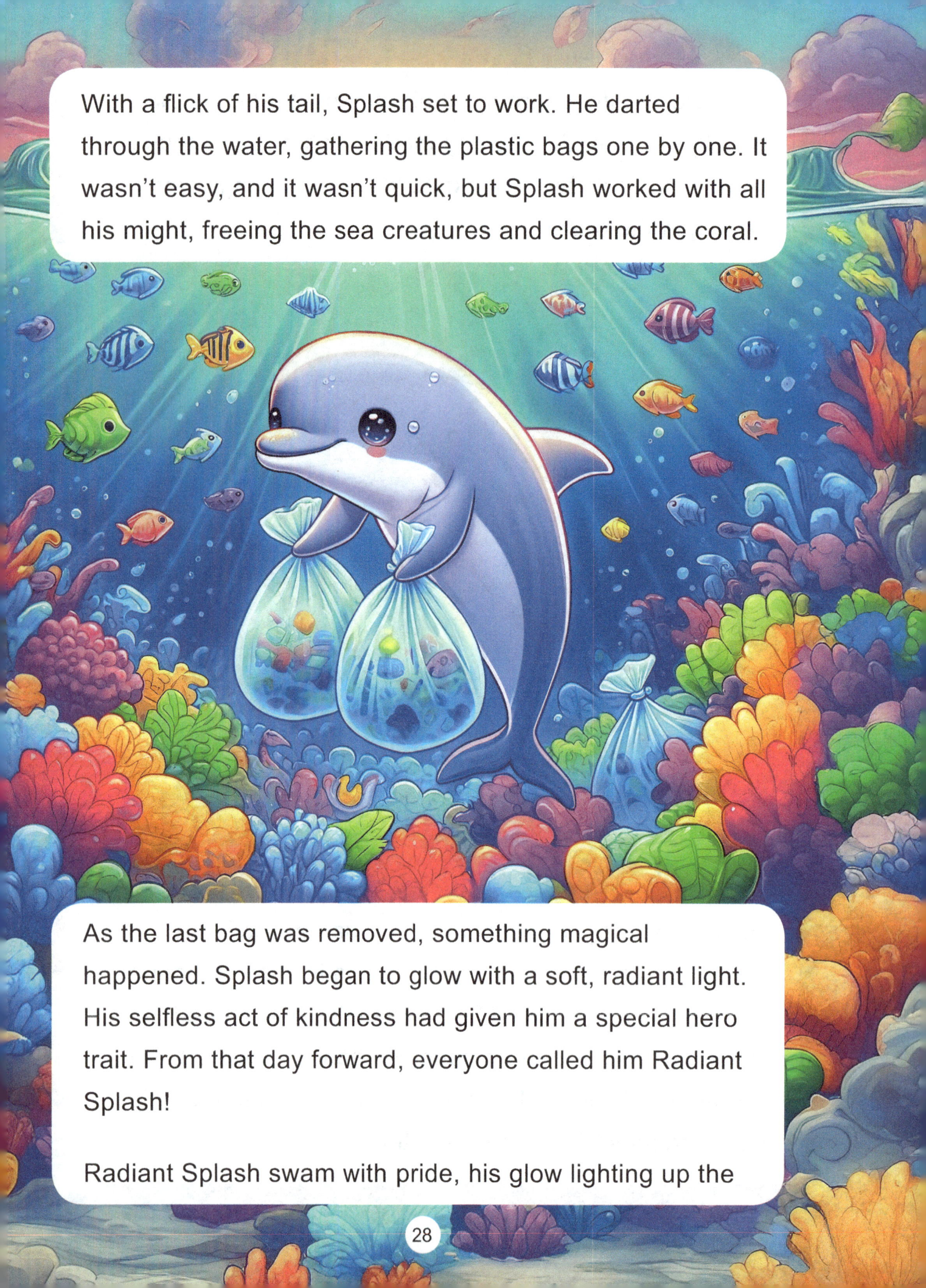

With a flick of his tail, Splash set to work. He darted through the water, gathering the plastic bags one by one. It wasn't easy, and it wasn't quick, but Splash worked with all his might, freeing the sea creatures and clearing the coral.

As the last bag was removed, something magical happened. Splash began to glow with a soft, radiant light. His selfless act of kindness had given him a special hero trait. From that day forward, everyone called him Radiant Splash!

Radiant Splash swam with pride, his glow lighting up the

ocean around him. His friends, inspired by his bravery and kindness, joined in, promising to help keep their underwater world safe and beautiful.

And so, Radiant Splash became not just a playful dolphin, but a true hero of the deep. His selfless act of putting the ocean's well-being before his own playtime taught everyone that true heroism shines through altruism. With a big heart and selfless actions, anyone can become a hero and illuminate the world around them.

The Heroic Helpers

A Story about Altruism

In the bustling town of Brightsville, where superheroes soared in the sky and battled villains with dazzling powers, a group of imaginative kids felt a little overlooked. They didn't have super strength or the ability to fly, but they had something just as powerful: big hearts full of kindness. They decided to become "The Heroic Helpers," donning capes and masks made from blankets and old clothes, ready to show the world that you don't need superpowers to be a hero.

One sunny afternoon, a mischievous villain named Chaos Carl descended upon Brightsville, turning the peaceful day upside down with his troublesome tricks. The superheroes were quick to respond, leaping and zooming to save the day. But amid the chaos, the littlest residents found themselves scared and confused.

That's when The Heroic Helpers sprang into action! They gathered everyone into a cozy, safe underground refuge that looked like a superhero hideout. There, they shared freshly baked cookies, wrapped shivering shoulders in warm blankets, and told stories filled with hope and courage. They even drew colorful pictures on the walls, turning the hideout into a magical place where smiles began to bloom like flowers in spring.

While the superheroes fought the villain above, The Heroic Helpers proved that kindness and care were their own kind of superpower. They made everyone feel safe and loved, showing that you don't have to fight villains to be a hero. Sometimes, a warm hug or a kind word is all it takes to save the day.

As the dust settled and Chaos Carl was whisked away by the superheroes, the town of Brightsville learned a valuable lesson. Heroes come in all shapes and sizes, and sometimes, the smallest acts of kindness are the mightiest of all. And so, The Heroic Helpers became cherished heroes in their own right, with the biggest hearts in all of Brightsville.

Chapter 4
Self-Control

Imagine you have a remote control that can manage your feelings. When you're about to get really mad, like when your brother takes the last piece of pizza, you press the "pause" button. That's self-control! It means choosing to stay calm and not letting your temper take the driver's seat.

For superheroes, self-control is super important. It helps them think clearly during sticky situations, like when a villain is causing chaos. Instead of getting angry, they take a deep breath, make a plan, and save the day with a cool head.

In your life, self-control is like having a superpower too. It helps you when you're feeling upset or frustrated. Maybe you want to yell or throw something, but instead, you count to ten, take deep breaths, or talk about what's bothering you. This keeps you in charge of your actions, making you a real-life superhero.

By using self-control, you can solve problems better, make friends easier, and feel happier inside. So, the next time you feel a big, stormy emotion coming, remember your superpower of self-control. It's a great way to show the world the superhero you are!

YOUR FUN CHALLENGE!

Your Mission: Next time you feel really excited, upset, or angry, try the "Pause and Stay in Control" Challenge. Before you act, stop for a moment, take a deep breath, and think about your next step.

Why? Pausing helps you make better choices, just like a superhero deciding the best way to save the day. Each time you do it, you're using your superpower of self-control!

Your Tracker: Each time you successfully pause and think before acting, fill in a box. Can you fill all 10?

☐ ☐ ☐ ☐ ☐ ☐ ☐ ☐ ☐ ☐

Remember: It's okay if it's hard at first. The most important part is that you tried. That's how you learn and grow stronger in your self-control. You're doing fantastic!

The Fiery Phoenix

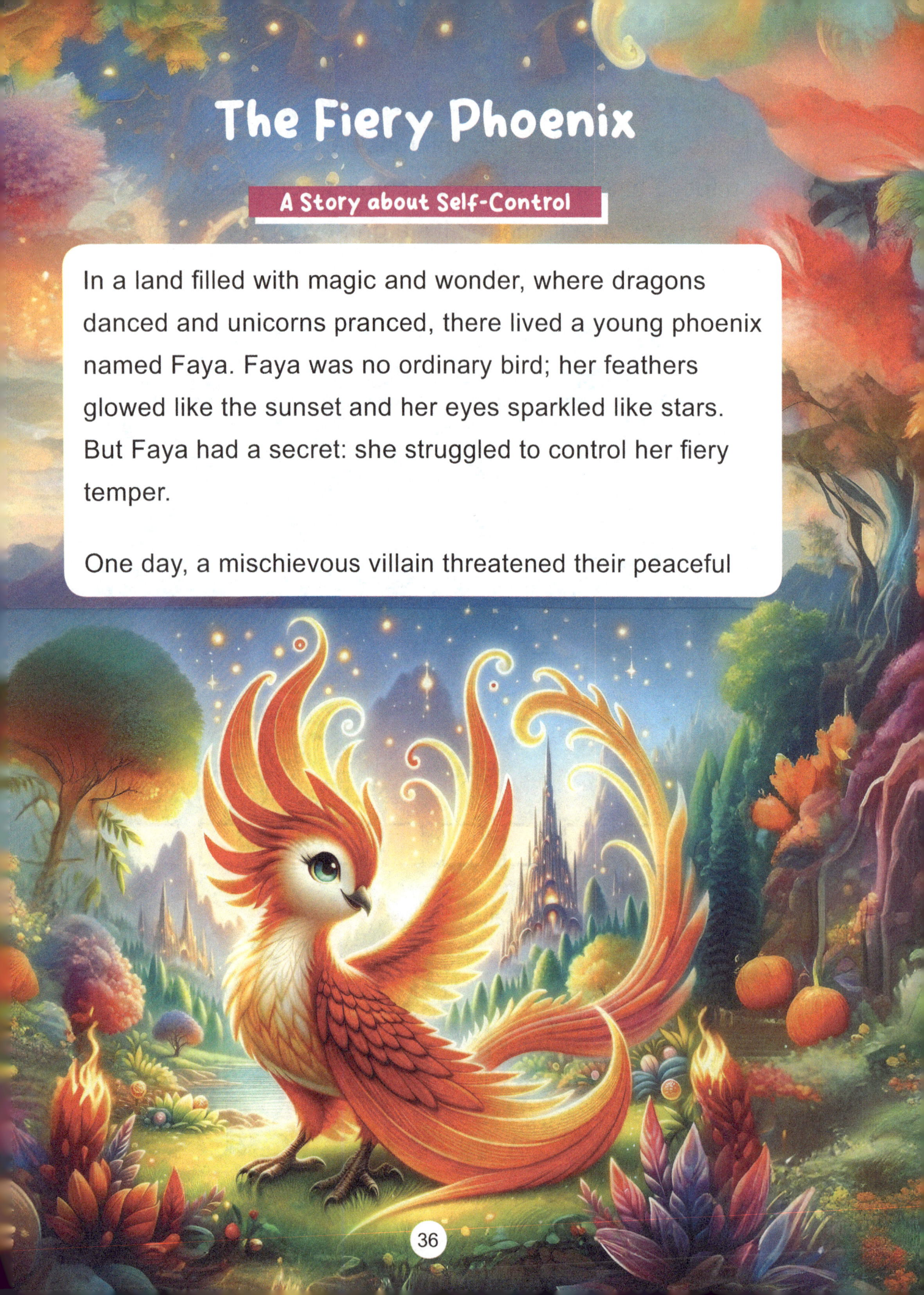

A Story about Self-Control

In a land filled with magic and wonder, where dragons danced and unicorns pranced, there lived a young phoenix named Faya. Faya was no ordinary bird; her feathers glowed like the sunset and her eyes sparkled like stars. But Faya had a secret: she struggled to control her fiery temper.

One day, a mischievous villain threatened their peaceful

realm, causing trouble and fear. Faya, wanting to protect her friends, became so angry that her flames grew wild and uncontrollable. Trees began to smolder, and flowers wilted under the intense heat.

The creatures of the realm, from the tiniest pixie to the mightiest dragon, gathered around Faya. They pleaded, "Please, Faya, you must calm your fire! Your anger might bring more destruction than the villain ever could."

Faya realized that her fiery temper was not only endangering herself but also her beloved home and friends. She closed her eyes, took a deep breath, and imagined her anger as a tiny spark that she could hold gently in her talons. With each breath, the spark grew smaller and cooler, until it was nothing but a warm glow in her heart.

With her flames now a gentle ember, Faya used her powers for good. She created a ring of protective fire around the realm that kept the villain at bay, and her warmth brought life back to the scorched earth, making flowers bloom and trees grow taller than ever before.

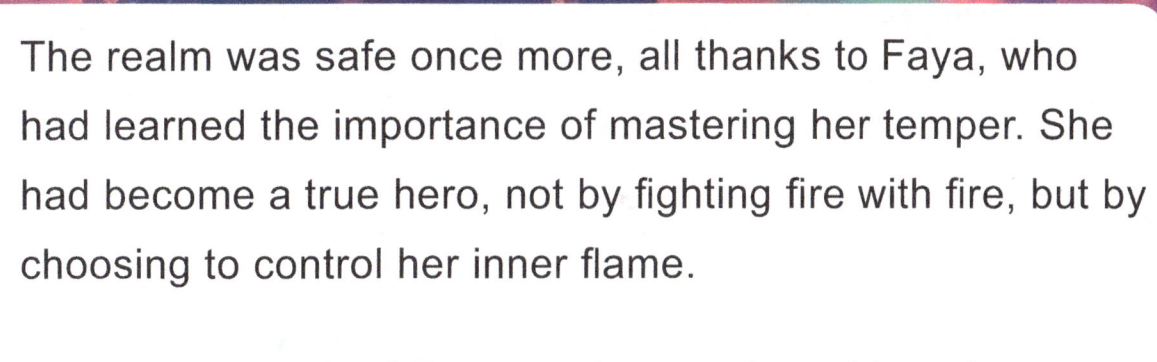

The realm was safe once more, all thanks to Faya, who had learned the importance of mastering her temper. She had become a true hero, not by fighting fire with fire, but by choosing to control her inner flame.

And so, the story of Faya teaches us that with patience and self-control, we can overcome any challenge and protect what we love.

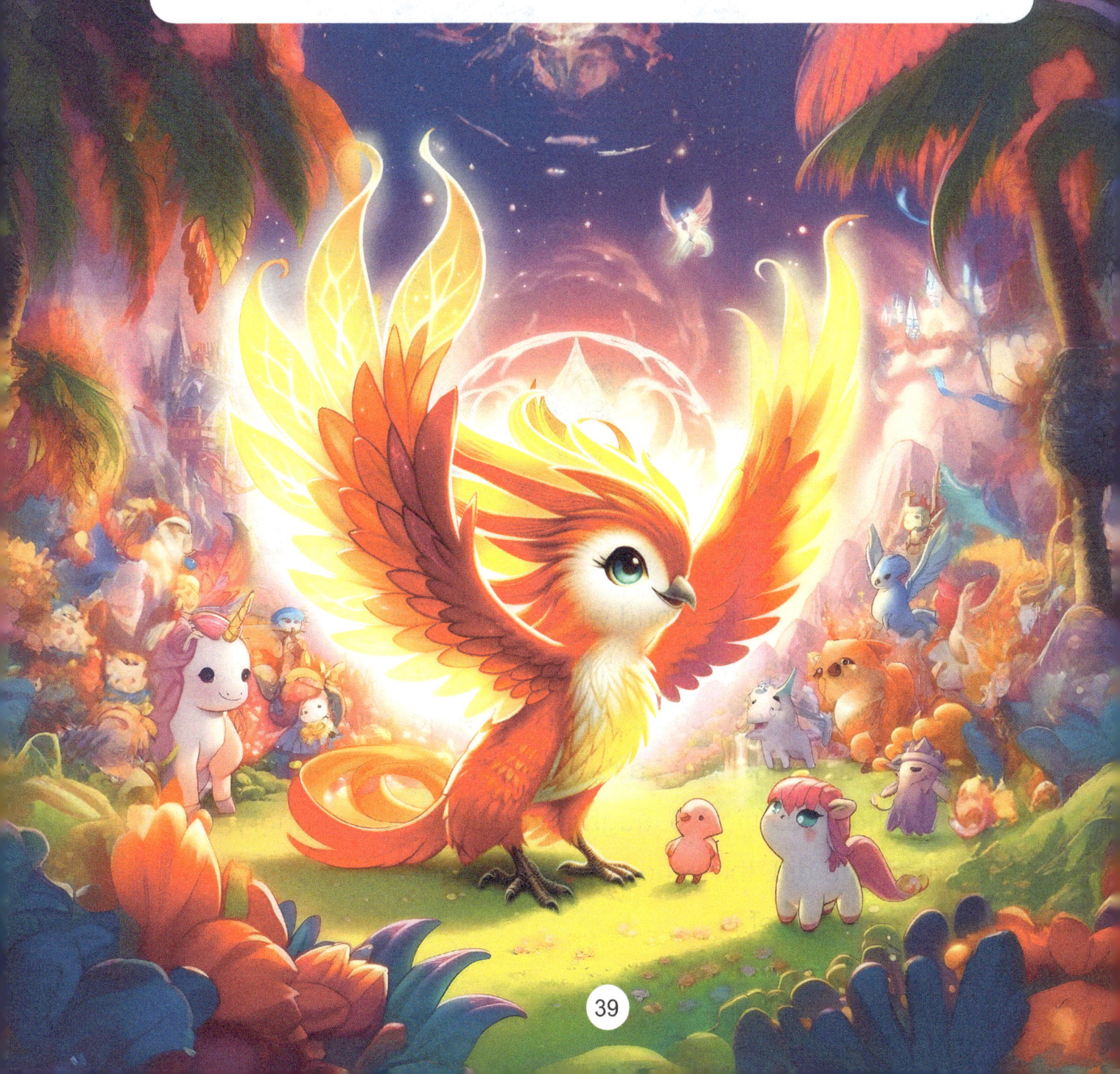

Layla the Wind Whisperer

A Story about Self-Control

Once upon a time, in a world where everyone had a bit of magic, there was a young girl named Layla. Layla had a special power – she could talk to the wind and ask it to do all sorts of things! But Layla was a bit like a whirlwind herself. She was quick to laugh and quicker to get angry, and when she did, the wind would swirl and twirl, causing all sorts of mischief.

One day, a sneaky villain named Tempesto came up with a naughty plan. He knew that heroes-in-training like Layla sometimes lost control of their powers. So, he stole Layla's favorite toy, hoping to make her so mad that her wind powers would create chaos.

And mad she got! Layla's temper flared, and so did the wind. It howled and roared, knocking over pots and sending hats flying. But amidst the chaos, Layla remembered what Grandma Fatima always said, "The greatest power is the power over oneself."

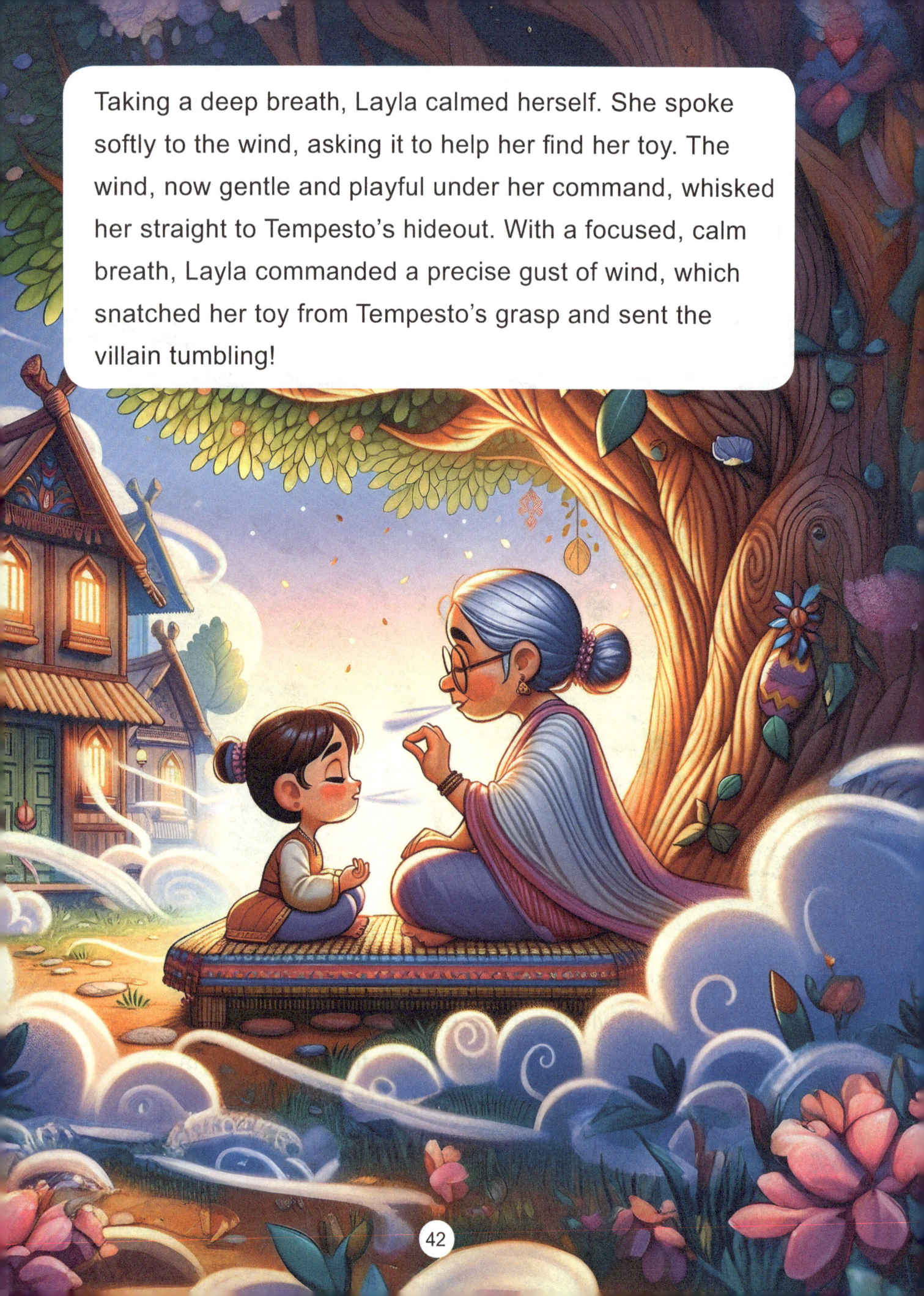

Taking a deep breath, Layla calmed herself. She spoke softly to the wind, asking it to help her find her toy. The wind, now gentle and playful under her command, whisked her straight to Tempesto's hideout. With a focused, calm breath, Layla commanded a precise gust of wind, which snatched her toy from Tempesto's grasp and sent the villain tumbling!

Layla learned that day that by mastering her emotions, she could control her powers better than ever. She became a true Everyday Superhero, showing everyone that the real strength comes not from the storm, but from the calm within.

And so, Layla and the wind lived happily ever after, swirling and twirling together, but always under control, ready to be the heroes the world needed.

Chapter 5
Cooperation

Imagine if a superhero tried to save the day all alone but couldn't lift a super heavy rock without a little help. That's where cooperation comes in! Cooperation means working together like a super team, where everyone helps each other to do something amazing that they couldn't do by themselves.

Even superheroes need buddies to team up with. When they join forces, they can outsmart the trickiest villains and save the world in ways one superhero alone could never do. It's their teamwork that makes them unstoppable!

For you, cooperation is like sharing your toys or playing a game where everyone has a role. It's important because, with friends by your side, you can solve tough puzzles, create magnificent forts, or win a game that seems impossible. By sharing your ideas and listening to others, you're not just being a good friend; you're being a superhero in your own world.

Remember, every time you work together with someone,

you're showing the world your superpower of cooperation. It makes every adventure more fun and every challenge a little easier. So, next time you're with your friends or family, think about how you can cooperate to make something awesome happen!

YOUR FUN CHALLENGE!

Your Mission: Invite someone to join you in an activity you usually do alone, like drawing or playing a certain game. (Each time, pick a different activity.) Or, ask to join in on something you usually don't, like cooking with your family.

Why? Working together is the superhero way! By inviting others or joining in, you're practicing your superpower of cooperation.

Your Tracker: Here are 10 boxes. Each time you cooperate in a different activity, fill in a box. Can you fill all 10?

☐ ☐ ☐ ☐ ☐ ☐ ☐ ☐ ☐ ☐

Remember: It's not about being the best; it's about working together and trying new things. That's how you become an everyday superhero!

Blue Rocket and the Falling Tower

A Story about Cooperation

Once upon a time, in the heart of a bustling city, there was a little superhero named Blue Rocket. With his bright blue armor, Blue Rocket was always ready to lend a helping hand, believing that with his strong arms and brave heart, he could handle anything all by himself.

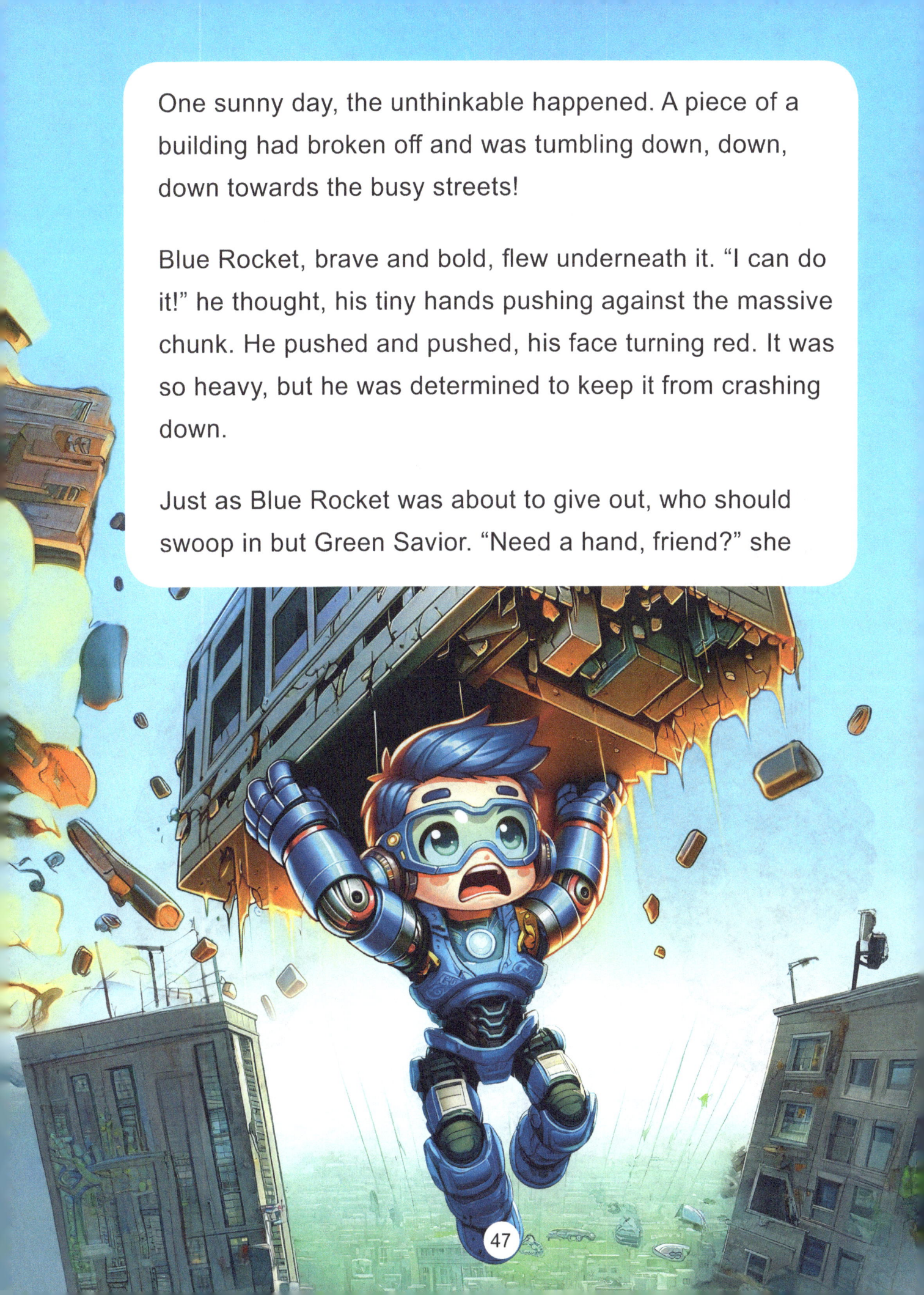

One sunny day, the unthinkable happened. A piece of a building had broken off and was tumbling down, down, down towards the busy streets!

Blue Rocket, brave and bold, flew underneath it. "I can do it!" he thought, his tiny hands pushing against the massive chunk. He pushed and pushed, his face turning red. It was so heavy, but he was determined to keep it from crashing down.

Just as Blue Rocket was about to give out, who should swoop in but Green Savior. "Need a hand, friend?" she asked, smiling kindly. With her strength, the weight seemed to become lighter.

And with a loud whoosh, Red Turbo appeared. "Teamwork makes the dream work!" she exclaimed, as she joined her friends.

Together, the trio formed a super team. Green Savior used her mighty strength, Red Turbo used her super speed to find the perfect spot, and Blue Rocket... well, he kept on pushing with all his might. They moved the piece of the building safely to an empty park, where it landed with a soft thud on the green grass.

The city cheered, and Blue Rocket learned an important lesson that day — the warmth of friendship and teamwork. "Thank you," he said, "for teaching me that some things can't be done alone. Together, we're not just stronger; we're super!"

And so, the three heroes stood side by side, their smiles as bright as the sun above, ready for whatever came next. Because now, Blue Rocket knew the true strength of a superhero was in the power of cooperation.

The Magical Light of Zara and Nia

A Story about Cooperation

In the twilight forest, where dreams whisper and magic dances in the air, lived two glowing fairies, Zara and Nia. They watched over the forest and its creatures, their lights a beacon of hope and guidance.

One moonlit evening, a baby unicorn named Unica found herself lost. Her tiny hooves trembled on the leafy floor, her eyes wide with worry.

Upon seeing Unica's distress, Zara and Nia flew down. "We must find her family in the north," Zara said, confident her direction was right. "No, they're in the south," Nia insisted, sure of her knowledge.

Without agreement, they split, creating trails of light in opposite directions. But oh, their separation confused Unica even more! She stood still, torn between two glimmering paths.

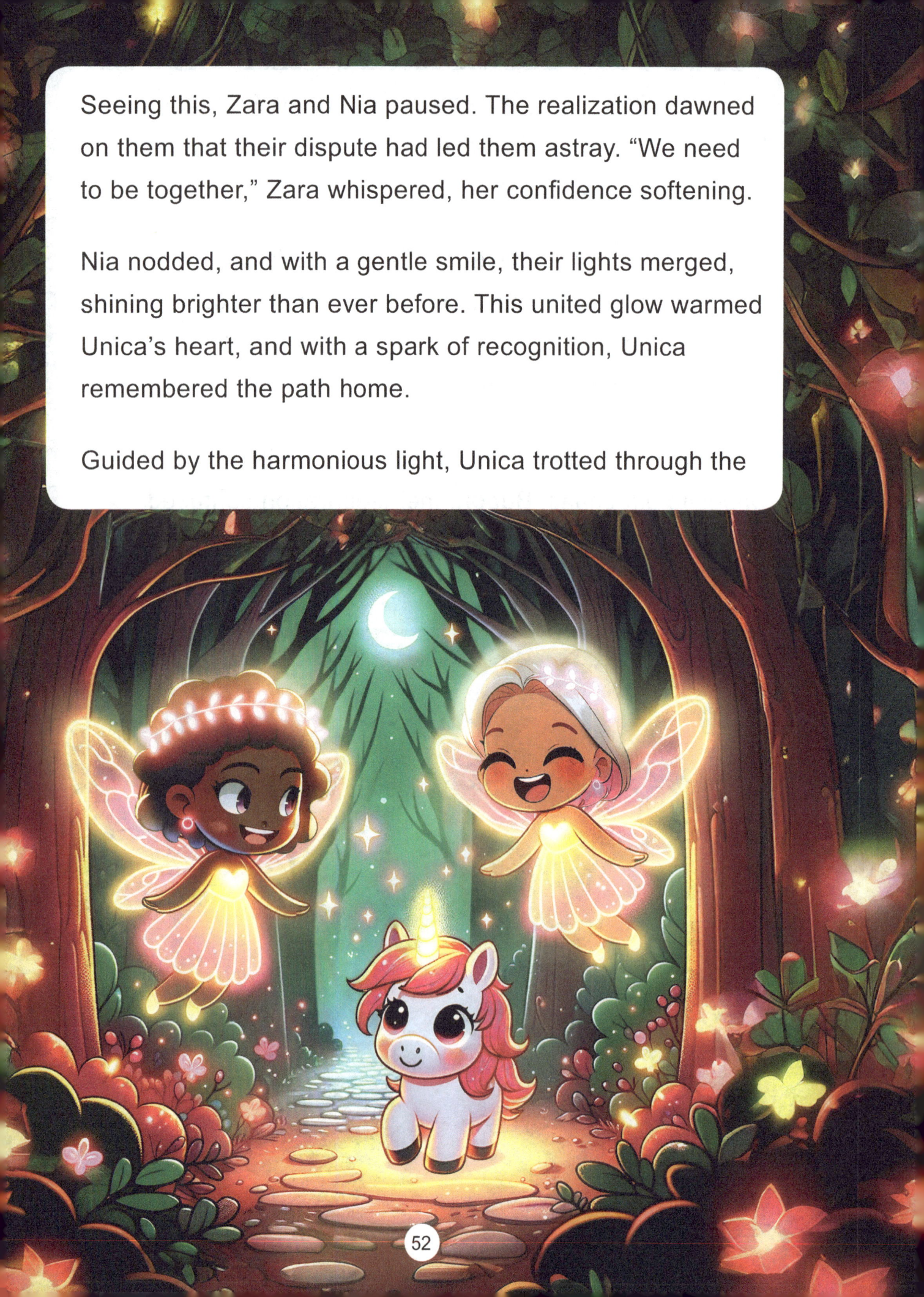

Seeing this, Zara and Nia paused. The realization dawned on them that their dispute had led them astray. "We need to be together," Zara whispered, her confidence softening.

Nia nodded, and with a gentle smile, their lights merged, shining brighter than ever before. This united glow warmed Unica's heart, and with a spark of recognition, Unica remembered the path home.

Guided by the harmonious light, Unica trotted through the

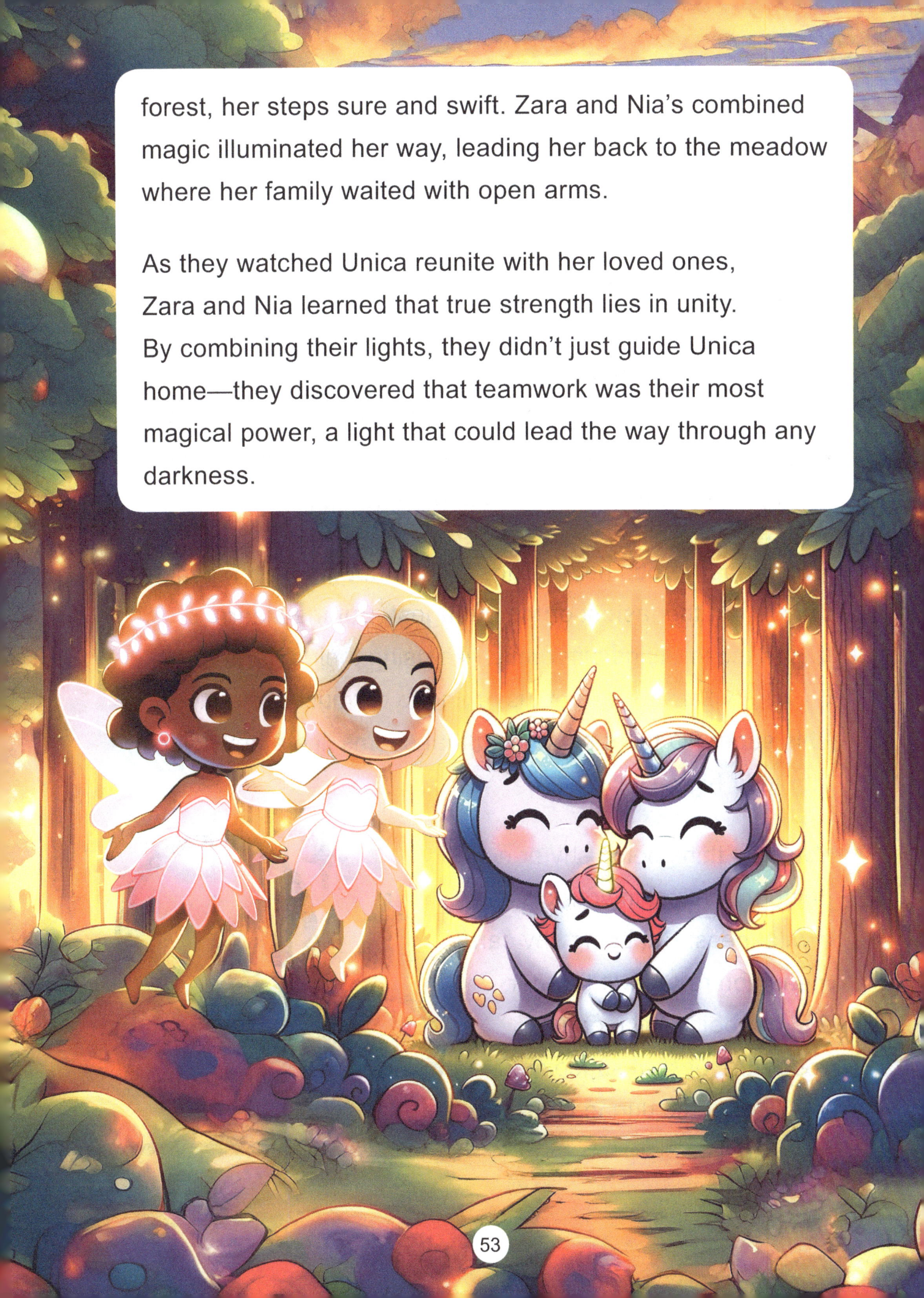

forest, her steps sure and swift. Zara and Nia's combined magic illuminated her way, leading her back to the meadow where her family waited with open arms.

As they watched Unica reunite with her loved ones, Zara and Nia learned that true strength lies in unity. By combining their lights, they didn't just guide Unica home—they discovered that teamwork was their most magical power, a light that could lead the way through any darkness.

Chapter 6
Turning Weaknesses into Strengths

Imagine you have a box of crayons, but instead of only your favorite colors, you find some you don't use much because they seem not as cool. But then, you discover those not-so-cool colors make your pictures pop and shine in ways you never imagined! That's a bit like turning what you think is a weakness into a super strength!

Even superheroes have things they're not good at. Maybe they're not the fastest or the strongest. But they learn to see these things differently, like using their smarts to outwit a villain instead of just trying to outmuscle them. This super flip turns something that seems like a downside into their biggest win!

You may think being shy or not being the tallest in your class is a weakness. But being shy can mean you're a great listener, and not being tall means you're the best at squeezing into tight spots during hide-and-seek!

Remember, superheroes and you too can turn any weakness into a strength. It's all about looking at it in a new, super way. This superpower helps you tackle challenges and shine brightly, turning you into an everyday superhero!

YOUR FUN CHALLENGE!

Your Mission: Find one thing you think is a weakness of yours, or ask someone what they think is theirs. Then, come up with a way to see it as a strength! For example, if you're super talkative, instead of seeing it as talking too much, think of it as being great at sharing ideas and stories.

Why? Just like superheroes, your so-called weaknesses can be your superpowers in disguise. This mission will help you see how awesome those unique parts of you can be!

Your Tracker: Here are 10 boxes. Each time you turn a weakness into a strength, fill in a box. Can you fill all 10?

☐ ☐ ☐ ☐ ☐ ☐ ☐ ☐ ☐ ☐

Remember: Every part of you has something special to offer. You're doing super!

The Goggles of Bravery

A Story about Turning Weaknesses into Strengths

In a little town where every kid dreamed of being a superhero, there was a boy named Ray. Ray wore big, round goggles to protect his sensitive eyes. But these goggles stood out, and oh, how he wished they didn't. He thought they made him look different from the superheroes he admired. He often wondered, with these goggles, could he ever be a hero like them?

One sunny day, without a whisper of warning, the sky turned a dusty orange. A wild sandstorm swept in, so fast and fierce that people didn't have time to run indoors. The world outside turned into a swirling, twirling haze of sand.

Ray, snug behind his goggles, could see through the sandy whirlwind. He knew he should rush home, where it was safe. But then, he saw Mr. Baguette, the elderly baker, looking lost and scared. Ray hesitated. "What would a superhero do?" he thought. And that's when Ray knew — he couldn't leave Mr. Baguette outside. It was up to him because his goggles made him the only one who could see.

Ray darted through the storm and guided Mr. Baguette by the hand. One by one, he found more people who were stranded and led them all to the gymnasium, the town's safe spot. Despite the relentless sand biting at his cheeks and the wind howling in his ears, Ray persevered, driven by the urgent need to ensure everyone's safety.

As the last person stepped into the shelter, Ray's heart swelled with pride. He realized that what he thought was a weakness was actually his superpower. His goggles weren't just goggles; they were his hero's gear, his very own cape and shield.

When the storm settled, the town buzzed with the tale of Ray who saved the day. Ray had become not just any superhero, but one who had learned that the things we think hold us back might just be the hidden strengths that let us soar.

Naldala's Invisible Quest

A Story about Turning Weaknesses into Strengths

In Emotia, a land where feelings could be seen, little Naldala's shyness made her invisible, a silent cloak she wore with a sigh, feeling it a burden rather than a gift.

Emotia was a place of wonder, where trees hummed with life and rivers giggled with clear water, all thanks to the twinkling Stone of Life.

But oh, a sly wizard with a heart like a prickly thorn had taken the Stone! He placed it beyond a long, narrow bridge, guarded by stern statues with laser eyes that zapped at any movement.

The village worried, "Without the Stone, our trees will droop and our rivers will hush." Naldala heard their frets and thought, "I'm invisible... maybe I can get past those zapping statues."

She tiptoed to the bridge under the moon's soft glow. The statues stood like sentinels, their eyes shooting beams at rustling leaves and night-time critters. But not at Naldala. She was as unseen as a secret, as quiet as a shadow.

Step by step, she moved across the bridge. The statues didn't see her; they didn't zap. Her heart danced a brave little jig — she was doing it!

Beyond the bridge, in the wizard's gloomy lair, there sat the Stone, dim and sad. Naldala, with a gentle touch, took the Stone and skipped back over the bridge. The statues stood silent, their eyes quiet, their lasers still.

Back in the village, with a cheer and a burst, Naldala appeared, holding the Stone high. It sparkled and whooshed, life swirling around it. Trees perked up, and the rivers sang once more.

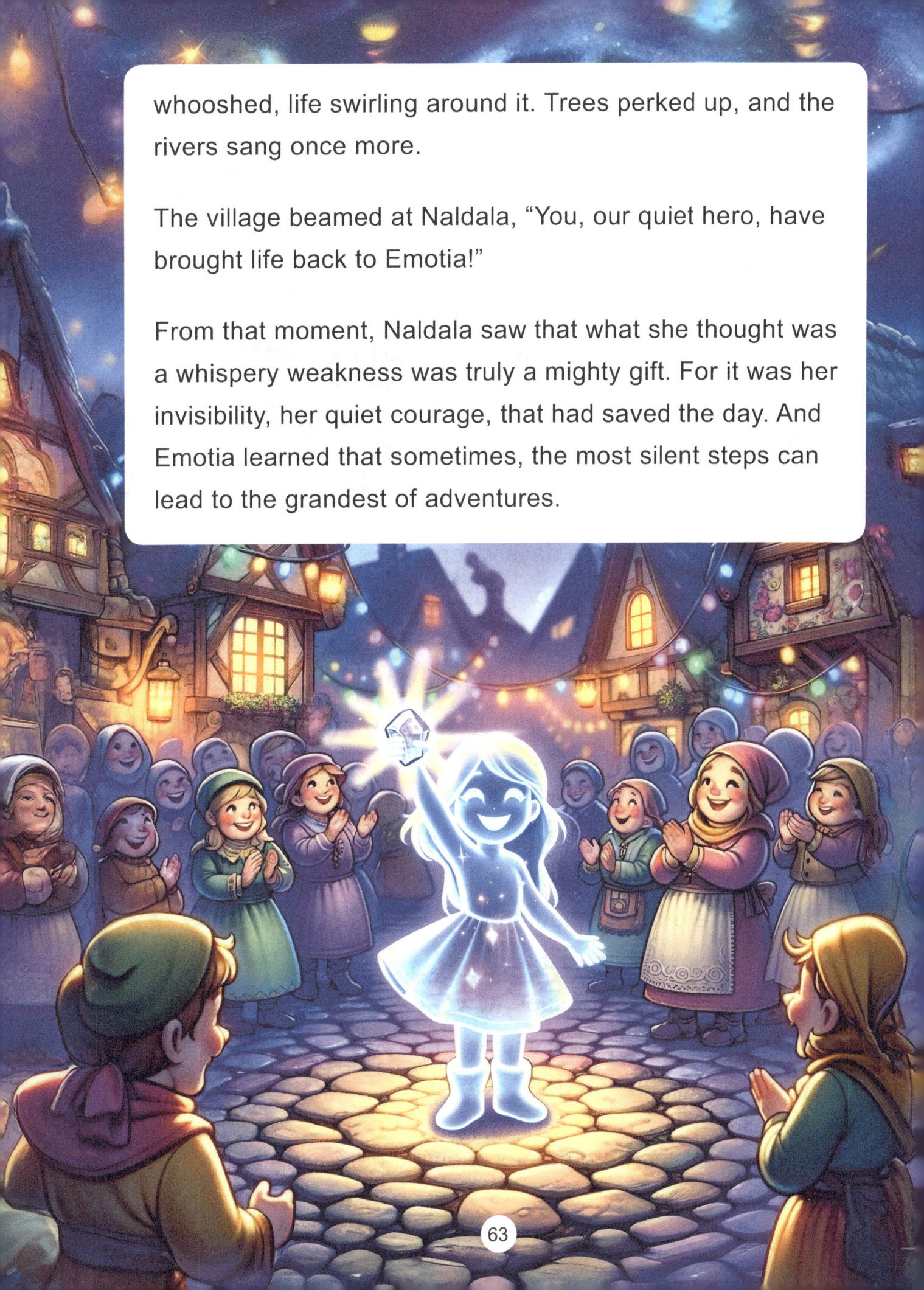

The village beamed at Naldala, "You, our quiet hero, have brought life back to Emotia!"

From that moment, Naldala saw that what she thought was a whispery weakness was truly a mighty gift. For it was her invisibility, her quiet courage, that had saved the day. And Emotia learned that sometimes, the most silent steps can lead to the grandest of adventures.

Chapter 7
Perseverance

Imagine you're building the tallest tower ever with your blocks, but whoops! Down it tumbles. What do you do? If you start stacking again, that's called perseverance. It's a fancy word for a simple superpower: never giving up!

Even superheroes have days when things don't go as planned. Maybe their super-gadget breaks or the villain seems too strong. But do they hang up their capes? No way! They try again, and then again, because superheroes know that every effort brings them closer to saving the day.

In your adventure, perseverance is your secret weapon. Whether you're learning to tie your shoes, read a book, or ride a bike without those extra wheels, sticking to it, even when it's tough, is your superpower. It's okay to stumble; what's important is you get back up and don't give up.

Being like a superhero means showing perseverance

every day. Each time you try and try again, you're getting stronger, smarter, and even more awesome. So, remember, when things get tricky, take a deep superhero breath, and say, "I won't give up!" Because that's what real superheroes do.

YOUR FUN CHALLENGE!

Your Mission: Whenever you feel like giving up on anything, try the "Just a Bit More" method. Before you stop, try to go on just a bit more. Whether you're trying to solve a difficult puzzle, finish your homework, or practice a new skill, give it that little extra push.

Why? This tiny step of doing "Just a Bit More" builds your perseverance muscle, making it stronger each time you use it. It's how everyday superheroes get better at what they do!

Your Tracker: Here are 10 boxes. Each time you successfully go "Just a Bit More," fill in a box. Can you fill all 10?

☐ ☐ ☐ ☐ ☐ ☐ ☐ ☐ ☐ ☐

Remember: Every moment you decide to continue just a bit more, you're taking a big step in becoming more resilient. This is what perseverance is all about. You're awesome for trying!

The Brightness of Darian

A Story about Perseverance

In a quaint village, shrouded in shadows by a curse from a villain who loved darkness, lived a young boy named Darian. Unlike any other, Darian had a special gift; he could glow, bright and warm, like a tiny sun. His dream was to chase away the gloom and fill his village with light, where laughter could echo freely, and fear would be but a memory.

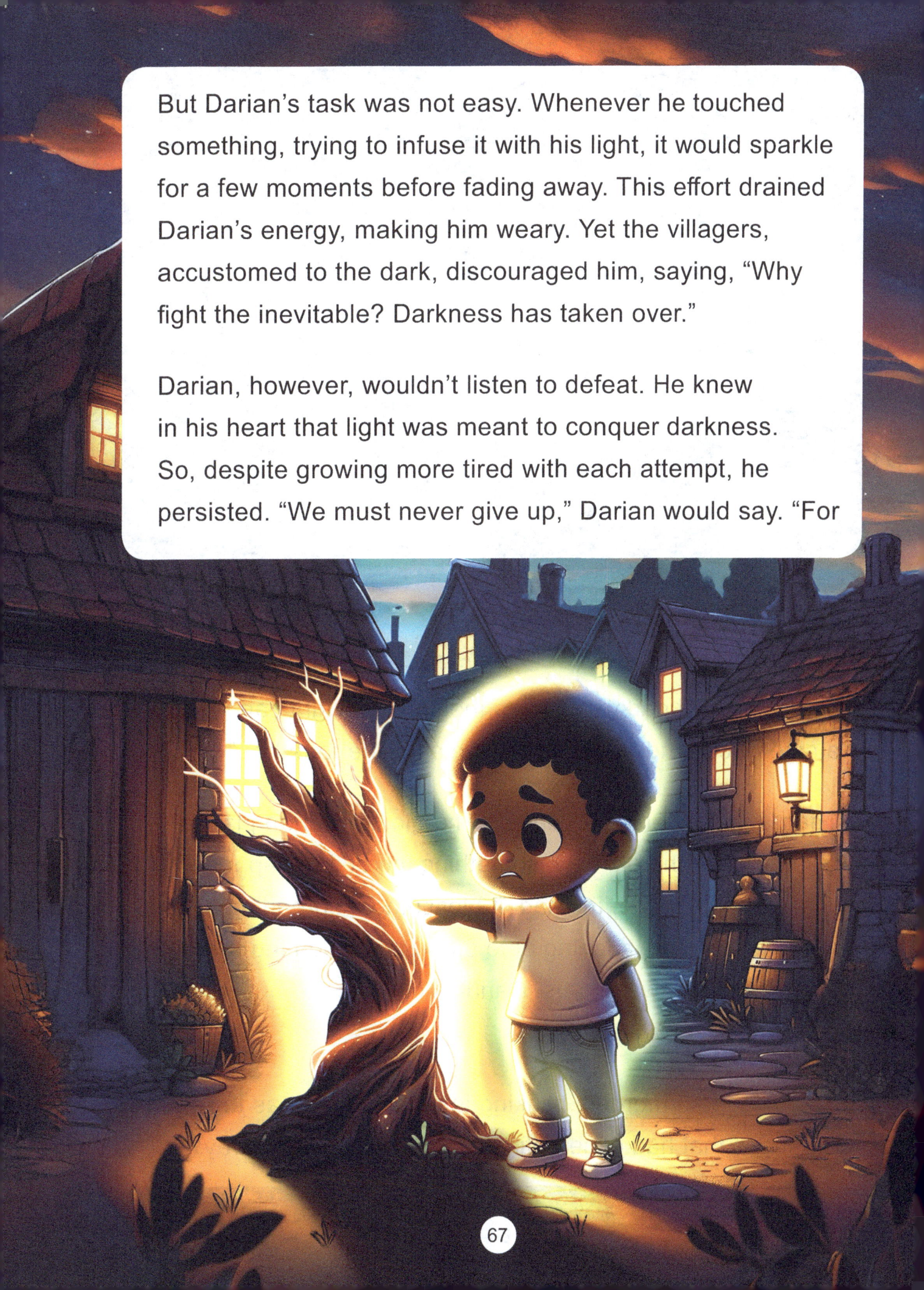

But Darian's task was not easy. Whenever he touched something, trying to infuse it with his light, it would sparkle for a few moments before fading away. This effort drained Darian's energy, making him weary. Yet the villagers, accustomed to the dark, discouraged him, saying, "Why fight the inevitable? Darkness has taken over."

Darian, however, wouldn't listen to defeat. He knew in his heart that light was meant to conquer darkness. So, despite growing more tired with each attempt, he persisted. "We must never give up," Darian would say. "For in the deepest darkness, even the smallest light can make a difference. And I believe we can all shine together."

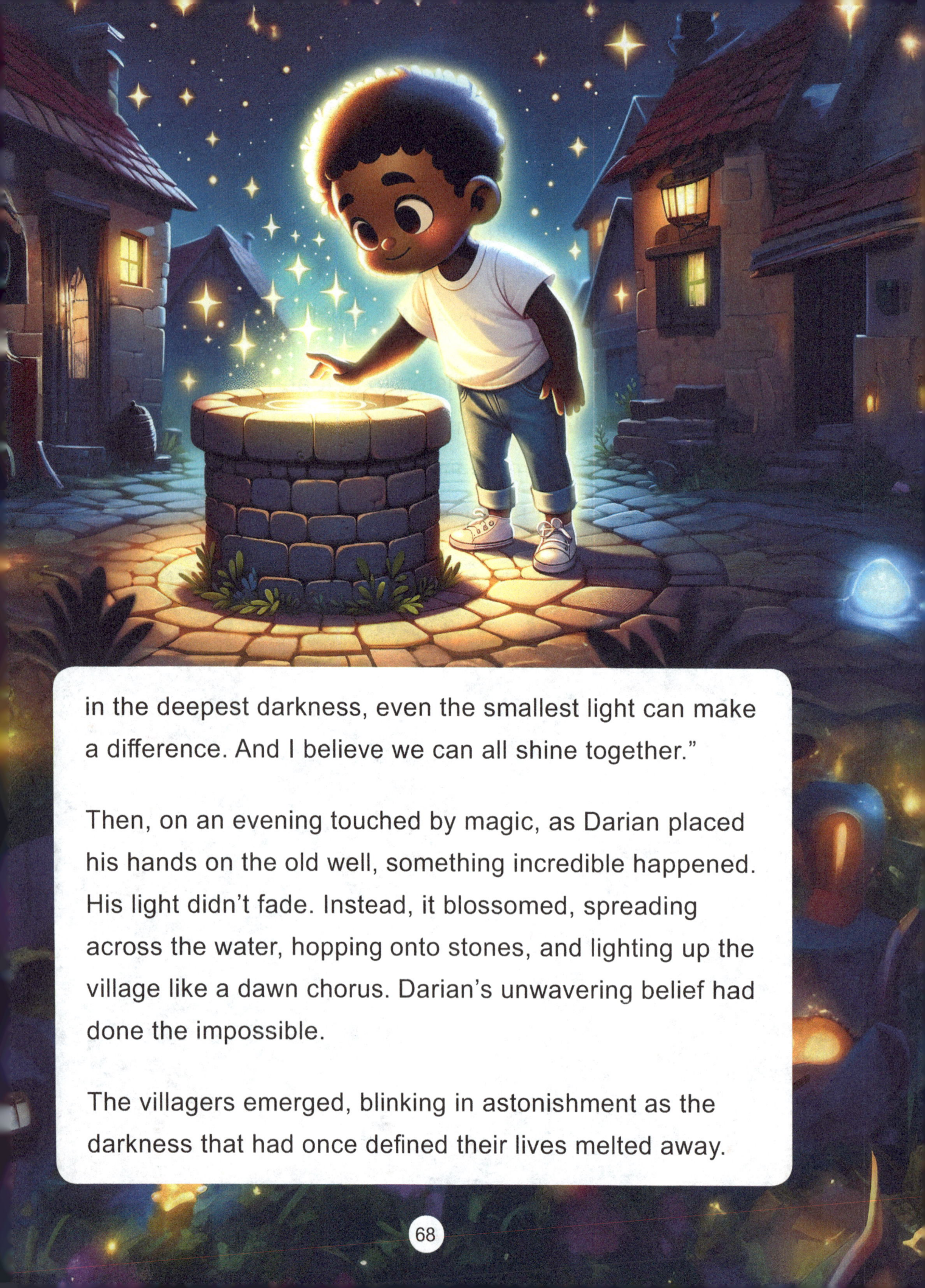

Then, on an evening touched by magic, as Darian placed his hands on the old well, something incredible happened. His light didn't fade. Instead, it blossomed, spreading across the water, hopping onto stones, and lighting up the village like a dawn chorus. Darian's unwavering belief had done the impossible.

The villagers emerged, blinking in astonishment as the darkness that had once defined their lives melted away.

Darian's relentless hope had illuminated not just their homes, but their hearts. Through his tireless efforts and his belief in the power of light over darkness, Darian became a true hero, teaching everyone the importance of never giving up, no matter how exhausting the battle may seem.

The Day Lucía Stood Again

A Story about Perseverance

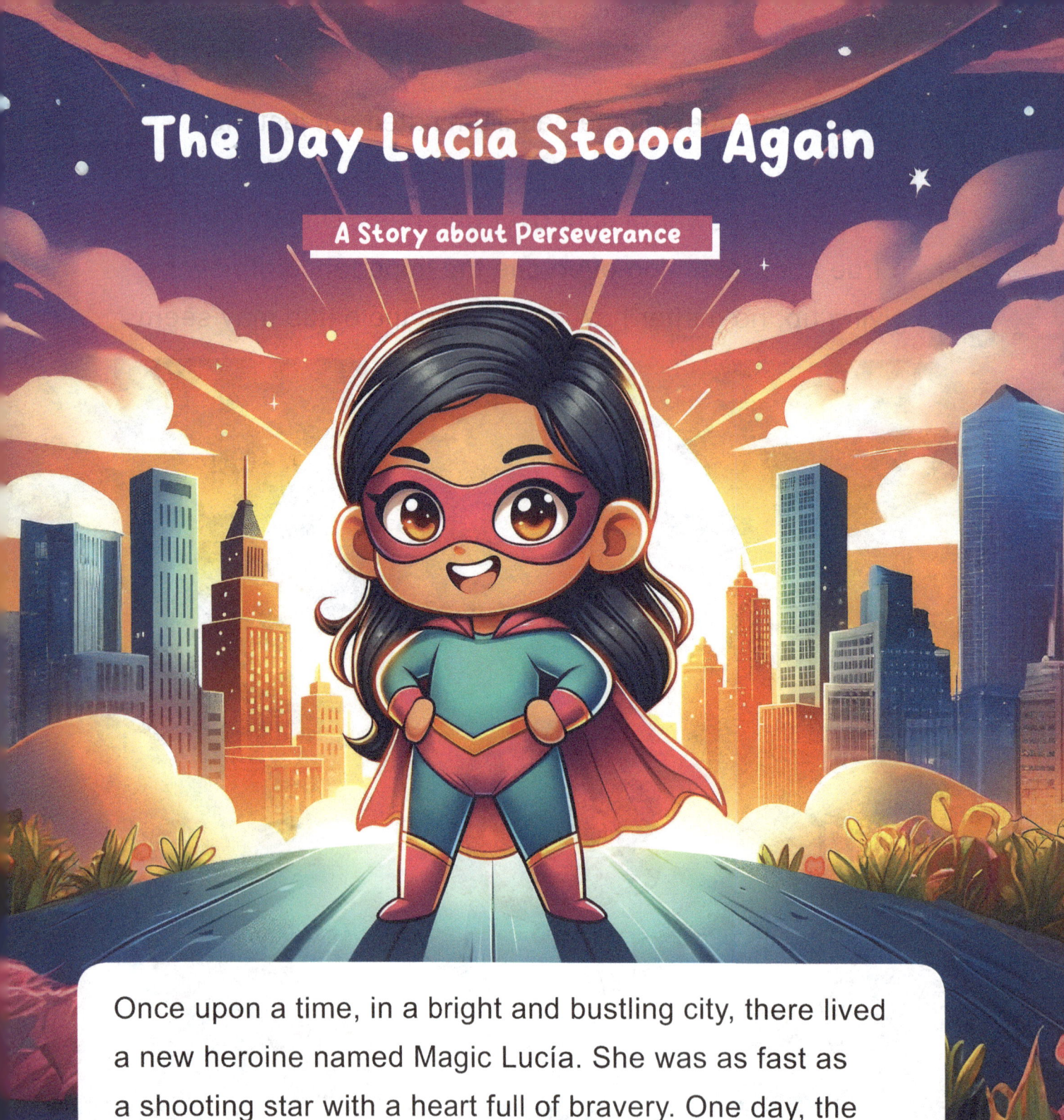

Once upon a time, in a bright and bustling city, there lived a new heroine named Magic Lucía. She was as fast as a shooting star with a heart full of bravery. One day, the villain Gloom Shadow started causing trouble, turning smiles into frowns.

Lucía, determined to save her beloved city, set out to battle Gloom Shadow. But oh no! She wasn't strong enough yet and stumbled. Gloom Shadow laughed and waited, thinking victory was easy.

Feeling down, Lucía thought, "Maybe I'm not cut out to be a heroine." But seeing the worried faces of the people, she remembered why she'd become a heroine: to protect people and spread smiles.

Taking a deep breath, Lucía said, "I may not be the strongest, but I have to try again. I refuse to give up!" She got up, dusted off her costume, and faced Gloom Shadow once more right away.

This time, as she stood before Gloom Shadow, she was scared but brave. They fought under the sun, Lucía jumping and sending flashes with all her might. Then, with a spirited leap and a flash of light, she took Gloom Shadow by surprise and defeated him!

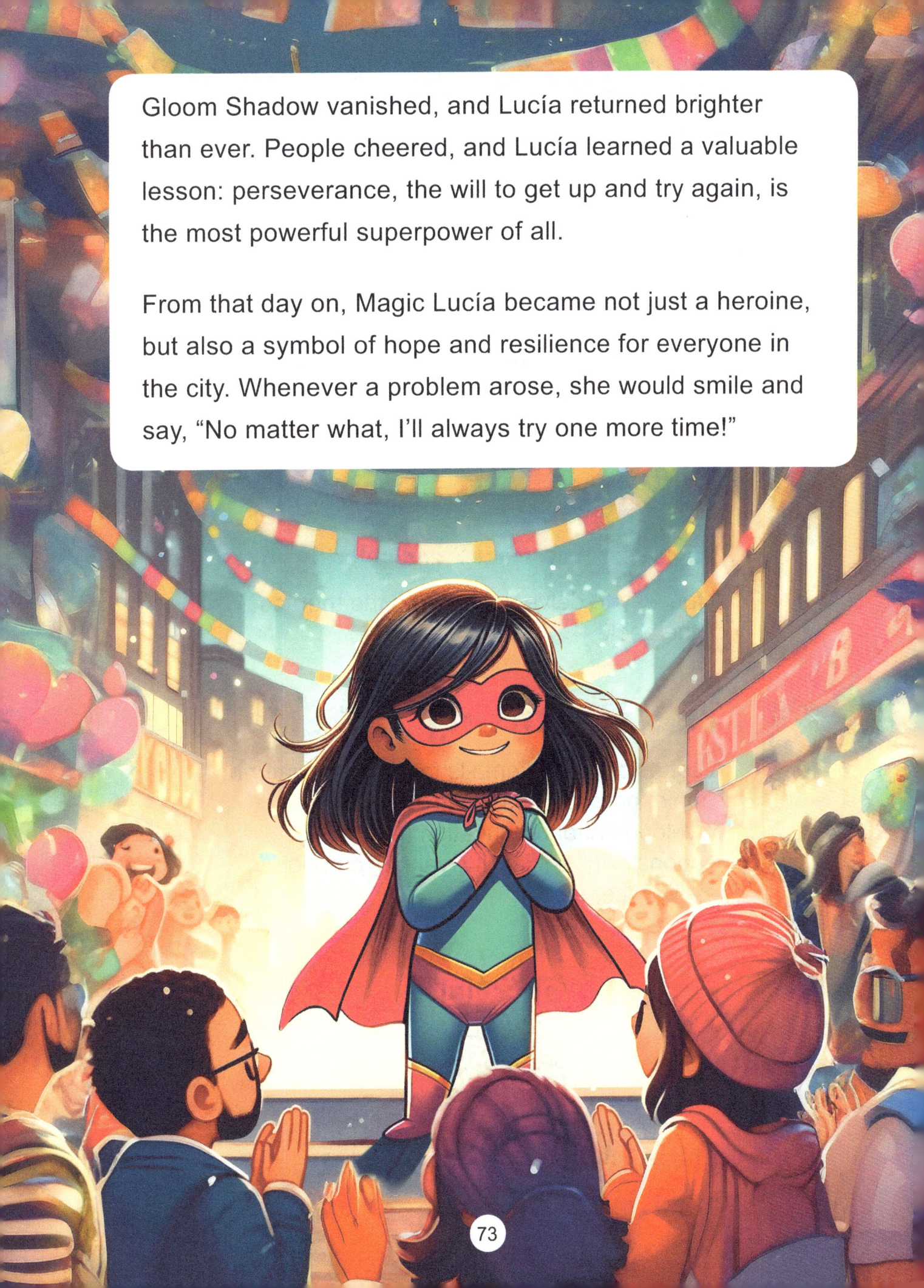

Gloom Shadow vanished, and Lucía returned brighter than ever. People cheered, and Lucía learned a valuable lesson: perseverance, the will to get up and try again, is the most powerful superpower of all.

From that day on, Magic Lucía became not just a heroine, but also a symbol of hope and resilience for everyone in the city. Whenever a problem arose, she would smile and say, "No matter what, I'll always try one more time!"

3 GIFTS FOR YOU!

1 **The Audio Version of This Book (in MP3 Format)**

Perfect for car rides, bedtime, or when parents are too busy!

2 **30 Pages of Activities!**
(Word searches, mazes, and coloring pages)

A fun way to delve deeper into the themes of the book!

3 **The "Parenting Tip" Emails!**

A series of weekly emails for parents featuring simple, practical tips to aid in children's development and education (autonomy, responsibility, sociability, values, emotional intelligence, etc.).

https://subscribepage.io/superhero

Made in the USA
Monee, IL
08 March 2025